A Variety of Passion

By

James L. Baumann

Copyright © 2012 Post Mortem Publications, Inc.
Second Edition 2014

All rights reserved. No part of this publication may be reproduced, stored in a retrieval system, or transmitted, in any form by any means, electronic, mechanical, photocopying, or otherwise, without prior written permission of the publisher. Published in the United States of America.

ISBN: 978-0-9839074-5-9

Library of Congress Control Number: 2012923398

Publisher's Note

For any questions concerning this publication or any other publications by the author, James L. Baumann, we invite you to direct your inquiries to us at:
Contact@Postmortempublications.com

This book of poetry is dedicated to

Wanda Klaas

Educator

For Inspiration

Forward

Often it is argued just how many styles, themes and forms exist when it comes to delineating the parameters of exactly what the nature of a poem is. I have found it to be a quite simple mathematical equation after all.

Once you calculate the totality of all of the emotions perceived to be felt by all living things and multiply that number by all of the possible causes that would create them in the first place and add to that every single living person's opinion and then subtract everything that has been heretofore written or expresses in any fashion about the subject of poetics and to that total you add the sum of one, -which is my opinion, and there you have it; the exact number. One. For each poem ever written is unique.

This collection is only a miniscule representation of the myriad of styles available that one could invoke in one's endeavor to find a commonality over a shared revelation of a natural truth in its simplest form.

Any thought provoked by this compendium will be its own justification, and I do thank you for your time.

James L. Baumann

> "Variety's the very spice of life,
> that gives it all its flavor"
>
> William Cowper
> The Task
> Book II
> The time-piece
> The argument
> Page 58
> Line 21-22

"To feel passion is to taste of the fruits of love."

-James L. Baumann

Passion

To feel passion is to taste of the fruits of love
Abandon ye all reason, to fly on winged doves
Taste the essence of ambrosia, sense the dare
You can smell the breath of sunshine in the air
It forces out the loathsome presence of despair

You can see beyond your selfish preservation
Acquire thoughts of ecstasy, be determination
Experience the energy you never knew before
Commit precociously, an act you can't afford
Dare to balance trust, submit before the Lord

Understand the gravity that spirits really fly
Embrace it candidly, your spirit's not inside
It's somewhere out there prodding you to be
Reject a rule embraced by mortals of insanity
For spirits fly translucently above impunity

What do they know of passion, all who die?
To only once have had it, is the reason why

Contents

The Rewards of Love 3
Enjoy Yourself 5
Ogden Bath 7
Honest Insincerity 8
A Spiritual Altercation 11
The Breath of Zephyrus 13
A Summers Eve 15
An Eggsoteric Eggschange 17
Ooh La La 19
Loria's Lament 21
An Angel's Inspiration 23
A Chilling Draft 25
There is No Middle Ground 27
Reflection 29
The Coffee Shoppe Bookstore 30
Capricious Beauty 33
Eggsestentialism 35
I Need a Drink 37
The Science of Slavery 39
Ode to Joyce 41
The Artist's Charge 43
A Mindful Experience 45
Really? 47
Experience Divinity 49
Chicken Anyone? 51
Forward 53
Is It True? 55
Bold Colors 57
Just One Look 59
Graduation 61
The Merits of an Honest Effort 63
To Dream Eternally 65

Pliant Convictions	67
A Solitary Tree	68
Diginnity	71
Hen Pecked	73
A Liquid Refreshment	75
To Have a Likeness to	77
To Scold Successfully	79
Oh, For the Love of Spud	81
The Joy of Salvation	83
The Rural Life for Me	85
To Taste Your Age	87
Think About It	89
The Write Advice	91
Degradation Incarnate	93
Fameininity	95
Inherent Independence	97
Excogitate Your Ride	99
Undying Love	101
A Whale of a Time	103
Heed in Deed	105
Fleedom	107
Optimism	109
A Full Palette	110
A Poet's Epitaph	113
An Irish Lassie	115
I Ain't an Ant!	117
The Snowman Cometh	119
L'eggalese	121
Prosperity	123
This Old House	125
You're Going Nowhere	127
The Omnipotent Book	129
Be Yourself, Damn It!	131
Eaten Alive	133
Hello	135

Souplexed	137
Darnel Knowledge	139
Poetry Can Be	141
Dogged Notions	143
Complete Surrender	145
The Hunk of Funk	147
Flight School	149
Sport	151
A Temporal Reception	153
Rampant Stupidity	155
Jeannie	157
With No Help From My Friends	159
The Legacy Left Behind	161
Reverent Elation	163
Wholly in Love	165
Treat Yourself	167
Hire Me!	169
Allured	171
Smokezy	173
Just Desserts	175
Trick or Treat	177
Vote Yourself a Job	179
The Complaint Department	181
To Nestle	183
Travel Arrangements	185
New Age Thought	187
Always	189
To Run Afowl	191
Standing Ground	193
Expose Yourself	195
A Fine Confection	197
Positively Fine	197
Finely Tuned	197
The Marriage of Mother Nature	203

Entreprendre

The Rewards of Love

It's nice to be in love with spring
To find the love in everything
Like feelings never felt before
The joy of youth upon your door

The summer sun bakes in the truth
That love goes on and passes youth
You know that love's the reason why
And pray that it will never die

Fall comes along with certitude
And love's true colors we conclude
Gives brilliance to our lives
And humbly hope as time goes by

When winter comes with its repose
A song of love will be composed

Enjoy Yourself

All his life he was a mountain man
Dreamed, he would be by the sea
Just lay there, right upon the sand
And tan himself for all eternity

The fisherman had dreams as well
To be beneath a mountain's majesty
To dwell on high, he felt compelled
And rest his bones beneath its trees

A professional, she thought she'd be
She figured that she had the time
Tenaciously, she gave up femininity
To battle hardened thoughts of mind

Your life, where it's not meant to be
Can cause your soul to be in agony

Ogden Bath

It is to laugh
When in the bath
You have your rubber duck

You splash about
Get water up your snout
As in the drain your toe is stuck

Your wounded pride
Is what the bubbles hide
With any kind of luck

Your fantasies abound
In a realm that you have found
That doesn't seem to suck

Your singing's such a wonder
That angels put asunder
You're very soul to pluck

The elusive soap escapes
As soapy mountains make
Your imagination run amuck

But the only thing that's real
That you can truly feel
Is that insipid rubber duck

Honest Insincerity

To breach sincerity, to give a speech to make another reach
Into the consternations of their soul for all to feel, in a shameless
Act of fraudulent duplicity, as plagiaristicly proclaiming
Pious grief is sad.

"I this" and "I that" abound in an oh-so-unprofound display of
True intention as to the orator's goal, to have you believe that
It is he or she, who most importantly, is the main attraction
For all to hail most reverently.

With props to astound and completely surround the staged event
It was most evident that the heavens had sent the plebs a
Seraphim to extol the struggles in their souls and to console the
Underlying fortitude they now behold.

Courageously the writers worked and searched to find a way
To perch the public servant above the rest of those who came,
To share and dare and publicly declare their own veracity,
Still unimpaired.

A band was sent, an accompaniment, that not only was meant
To enhance, but also to romance the dance, that was to be
Conducted and then to be instructed by one entrusted to
Deliver the goods as true and unadjusted.

Unprincipled, the "I" became "we" from one who had not
The dignity to write the eulogy from inspiration; relying on a
Writer who is patiently much brighter, but also lacks a decent
Ethical foundation.

The ceremony went on as planned and food a-plenty was
At hand to nourish all the minds demanding closure, and in
Sympathy and empathy the spoken words quite lyrically
Were heard with great exposure.

As all things come to pass, the end appeared at last, and
In finality they all went home that day, to wrestle quite
Concernedly, with the way the ritual had portrayed their
Feelings that were flayed, for all to see, for all eternity.

The only honesty revealed, as it showed up unconcealed,
When all the hands were shook that day, the poignant
Question asked, of all the folks that were amassed, was
"Do you think my speech was good today?"

A Spiritual Altercation

I need to know the reason why
The breath of nature whispers
To me while I think and sigh

Under the sun that blisters
Me with great intensity I feel
Perhaps that I should know

A reason why the Son's ordeal
Intently failed in faith to show
Some mercy for my plight

For hail to Thee, blithe spirit
That whirls around Your might
Perchance You cannot hear it

The answer is, - there is no why
As God and Nature doth collide

The Breath of Zephyrus

As beauty is love for all to have and to hold
A single thought, unique to one's own soul
It takes away a young man's breath to see
A summer cotton dress, fluttering aimlessly

Oh wind, you know exactly what to do
To give a man such passion he'll peruse
The sound of laughter and a sunny smile
To chase a dream, his very will beguiled

With hopes of being caught she flits along
With flowers in her hair she sings her song
To consummate her purpose is her goal
With love and tenderness to make her whole

Look now! A sprite has beckoned unto me
Fore she fades away this day, for all eternity

A Summers Eve

As one surveys the sunset's creamy crimson sky
That had caught the night before it closed it's eyes
And just when it's eastern half
Had turned the swirling clouds at last
Into a faded hue of royal blue
It left them there to dissipate and die
And in life's vanity you wonder why

An Eggsoteric Eggschange

The chickens understood
There is safety in a flock
And created Chickenhood
To avoid a chicken crock

Turkeys weren't invited
Regarded to be dumb
The chickens all united
To vote them out as one

And so the Turkey Club
Refusing to be beaten
Reminded Chickenhood
Our eggs are never eaten

Ooh La La

There is nothing like a French girl to make a boy a man
Especially in springtime when Chauvin makes his stand
To feel the conquest of desire, within his heart he tries
To find the right selection, a fancy to his very eyes

He banters all about the town to find a medal for his chest
There is no way he wants to settle, just for a second best
He wonders just exactly, how much it's going to take
To sacrifice naiveté, …his prideful dignity at stake

He chooses trepidatiously and hopes she won't discover
His undisclosed ineptitude, his weakness as a lover
With charm and femininity, with softness to the touch
Her scent has overcome him, he surrenders in the clutch

He'll never be the same again, he'll know no greater joy
For there is nothing like a French girl to make a man a boy

Loria's Lament

Technically, I went to work today
Methodically, I sat and then I prayed
Eventually, my faith had been restored
Mechanically, my task and was my reward

The mother of all files sat on my desk
And challenged me to do my very best
I summoned all my love and intellect
To keep the pleasant face I must reflect

This task is just a task and is inanimate
This job will never be compassionate
I don't know what I'm worried about
It's finished when this deadline's out

Although I love my job to death
At times it takes away my breath

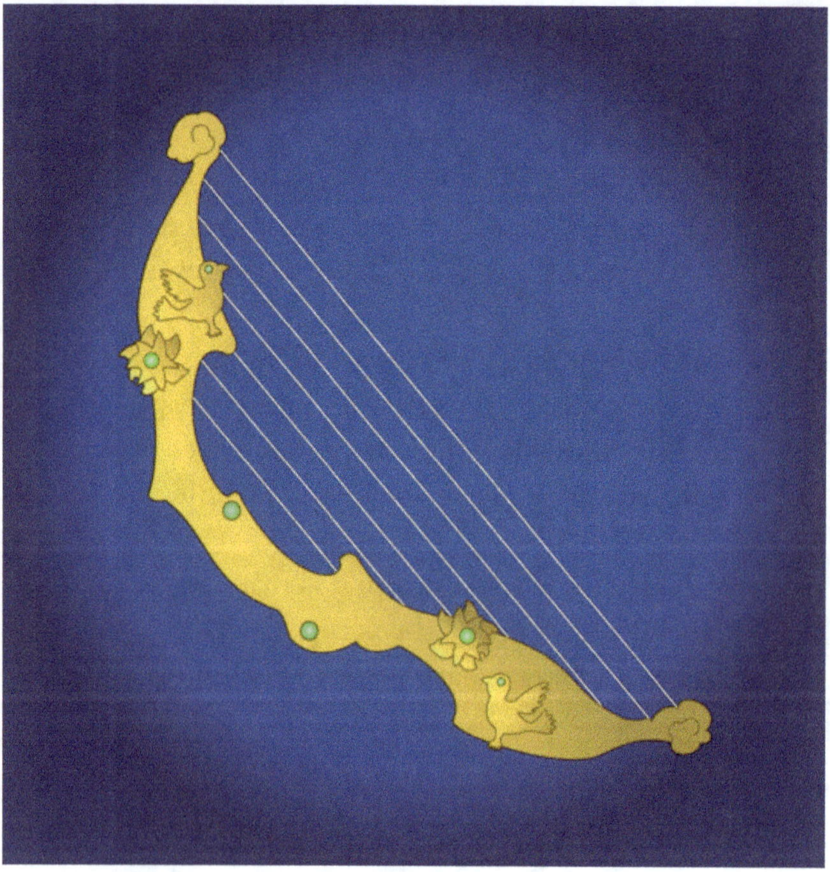

An Angel's Inspiration

At Christmastime we hear the angels sing
With golden harps, they play on silver strings
They harmonize our souls in dulcet song
And in our loneliness, they tell us we belong

To things much greater than ourselves to be
Discovering the very soul of our own mortality
We name them after senses, we can only feel
In heartfelt thoughts, no longer unconcealed

The sanctity of my conviction, I affirm as true
And realize that Herald Angels brought me you
To verify and certify a meaning in my strife
In terms of love and ecstasy, you are my life

Eternally you make me whole
You sanctify my very soul

A Chilling Draft

The summer's heat was in full force
As Caesar's August took its course
Upon the weak and old

As for the strong and young at heart
The summertime is best to start
The conquest of a soul

Having aspirations to behold
And honored duty, blatantly sold
For pocket watches made of gold
For eager minds to be controlled
To make a man to be so bold
To give his life to fit the mold

Of a politician - is oh so very cold

There is No Middle ground

Wednesday comes and Wednesday goes
And I wonder if anyone knows
That it actually exists

It's sad to see the day go by and then to sigh
It's gone forever now and not care why
To never, ever have it missed

I struggle in the middle of the week
A reason to continue on and seek
A meaning for my strife

On Monday, I had plotted and I planned
To be successful, throughout the land
And recognized as great

On Tuesday, I went to implement my deeds
My zeal still unencumbered to succeed
In adding fame to my estate

On Wednesday, all I did was work all day
I had no time to stop and play
No one even noticed me

On Thursday, I began to wonder why
The day before had gotten by
Without a cry so stealthily

On Friday, I had realized my fate
It is those Wednesdays no one can escape
For it's the grind that crushes you

Reflection

No one poetifies in rhyme anymore
No one takes the road to Rome
They take a jet

They fly through the clouds
Of obsequious verbiage
So tell me

What do they get?

A muddled mind perhaps is all
When taking off
Or landing

It is the sky that makes the cloud
Just wonder why
It floats

For those who cannot understand
The purpose of the cloud
Creating all the chaos

It is to sire harmony

The Coffee Shoppe Bookstore

Blue eyes twinkled as they opened
And saw the void
Their head was in a wicker basket
That sat upon a feathered bed

They peered about as if annoyed
And wondered why they were not dead
Is that a cactus that I see?
The head thought
Is that a flower? How could it be?
With all those thorns about?

The leafless tree that threw no shadow
Anywhere was silent
I asked it how it had got to be
It only stood there in-compliantly

A lizard here, a lizard there, a landscape
That was not so bare
That I had felt that I was all alone

There was a fly that had no wings
A rusted car that lacked the things
To make it go

There was a lover's heart which beat itself
Upon a rock with such conviction
That it never, ever, ever stopped

There was a noise throughout the air
It was hard to hear, but it was there
It was a song that had no ear to make it be
Discordantly it dared to sing for all eternity

A wafting smell had caught my eye's attention
It smelled of bread

I do not know if you have been here long
But as for me, - I arrived by chicken

Capricious Beauty

Pick me, Pick me, She hoped and hoped in desperation
I want to be the one, I want to be the one!
She petitioned and She prayed, in a wanton declaration
I want to be the one, I want to be the one!

Then there were plenty more who prayed and prayed
She's not the one, She's not the one!
As single mindedly they all conveyed and all relayed
She's not the one, She's not the one!

So in finality and in reality, a victory is now declared
Yes, She had won,… Yes, She had won!
The crown is Her's, and Her's alone to bear and wear
For She had won, Yes,… She had won!

As heavy is the head that wears the crown might be
The heavy hand of fate, - is found to be a fickle She

Eggsestentialism

I came first said the chicken
But the egg could not reply
With silence it was stricken
Too young to argue why

Then after chicken school
The egg now disavowed
It's thoughts as minuscule
Dismissed as unprofound

Attending Hen University
Much wiser she uncovered
That life is not an adversity
It's a mystery to discover

I Need a Drink

Prudence was her given name
And justice was her driven game
For all who played before her in her court

As blind as a bat, she sat and sat
With her rules so pat and her judgments that
Only a fool would support

The people paid to see, before them on TV
And on their copied DVDs,
A just decree, denouncing inhumanity

But as the motions were filed, so came the denials
As the ritual of trial
Was now in the style of complete insanity

How much does it cost to have won but have lost
Your dignity tossed
Right into the sauce, that creates the swill of society?

As the bank accounts rise
Off some poor bastard's demise,
One can only surmise, there is just no such thing as sobriety

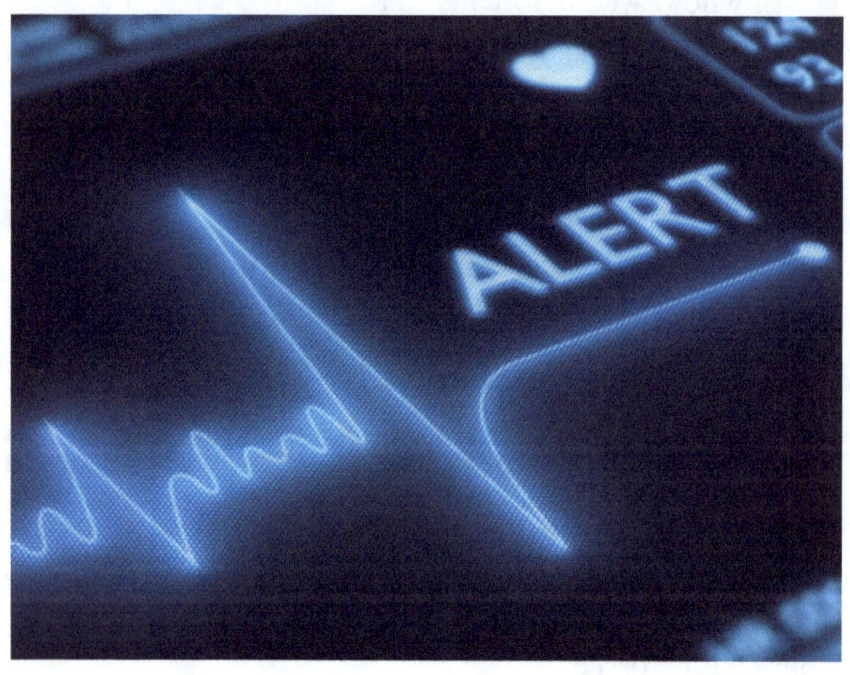

The Science of Slavery

I was compromised beyond my will to be
It had crept inside me, while I was asleep
Each day it took a little task away from me
My constitution ran away without a peep

At first I thought it would enhance my state
For I could go beyond my physical plane
Transform myself above my worldly fate
To leave behind my cumbersome complaints

It isn't the alcohol that I cannot resist
It isn't cigarettes or food that beckons me
It's not cocaine or crack, I must insist
For my addiction is acclaimed most socially

But since I am the jailer, locking me inside
If I become plugged, will only my computer die?

Ode to Joyce

I think that it will always stand
A poet's tribute to a man

A man who's hungry as a man
To be as tough and rugged as he can

A man who looks to God all day
And for the weak and poor he prays

A man who stands for right and wrong
To only independence he belongs

Upon his brow a righteous burden sits
To never weaken and he never quits

For poems are made to understand
That only God can make a man

The Artist's Charge

When poetry defines the poet
As art defines the artist
Does inspiration really show it
Or is their truth the farthest
Thought within their minds

Rhythm, rhyme and meter are but rules
Paint and clay and canvas are but tools
To help the spirit of the work prevail
The verity of its message must entail
The soul within it's times

The song of life belongs to one and all
Composer and conductor matters not
To give a pound of flesh is small
So sacrifice in deed becomes your lot
To be within your kind

For creativity is born alone
God's gift unto the artist's soul
For it's a sin to sell for gold
A precious gift you do not own

Am I my brother's keeper?

A Mindful Experience

It was only yesterday since I returned
From an excursion I had truly earned
By saving up the little things I cherish
Wisely using them before they perish

I visited a place, I've never been before
Quietly secluded, next to a sandy shore
A mighty mountain's majesty on high
Gave added brilliance to a summer sky

The magic lights of a sultry city night
Are mindfully emblazoned in my sight
As vividly I do recall and duly swear
I witness to it all, for I was truly there

The inspiration of a dream was all it took
To testify that I was there, inside the book

Really?

Happiness cannot be punished

Satisfaction is a slice of peace

A pane of glass has no color

Beauty transcends the ugly

The whole is always bigger

A destination is not an end

Nothing is always smaller

A straight wall is sterile

To belong is temporary

The wind is never still

To love is to be aware

Hope bears no action

A spirit has no form

Life is always alive

Faith is all soul

Time is not

Poetry is

Life is a glass of champagne

Experience Divinity

Shakespeare wrote of death and love alike
Spencer scripted godly love in angel form
Ms. Browning surly gave us love's delight
While Frost decided difference conforms

Shelly revealed a mighty King's despair
While Milton brought us virtue to admire
Keats romanced a joy beyond compare
Byron's shores of freedom wrought desire

Dante Alighieri quested after love divine
Donne epistolized where holiness survives
Millay bore witness as to her pain sublime
Mr. Browning tried to capture death alive

Poets pass away, but their sonnets it is said,
Resurrect them every time their poem's read

Chicken Anyone?

The sky is going to fall
The chicken did proclaim
It will fall upon us all
Fat and skinny all the same

I must warn everyone
To get themselves prepared
For soon the day will come
And no one will be spared

The little chicken cried
And warned capriciously
If I'm going to end up fried
I'm going most deliciously

Forward

What have I done?
I've left my home
I'm only one
And all alone

My home is now
Just bygone news
I don't know how
To cure the blues

I can't return
It's not the same
For I have learned
A different game

To say a prayer
For I'm not there
Anymore

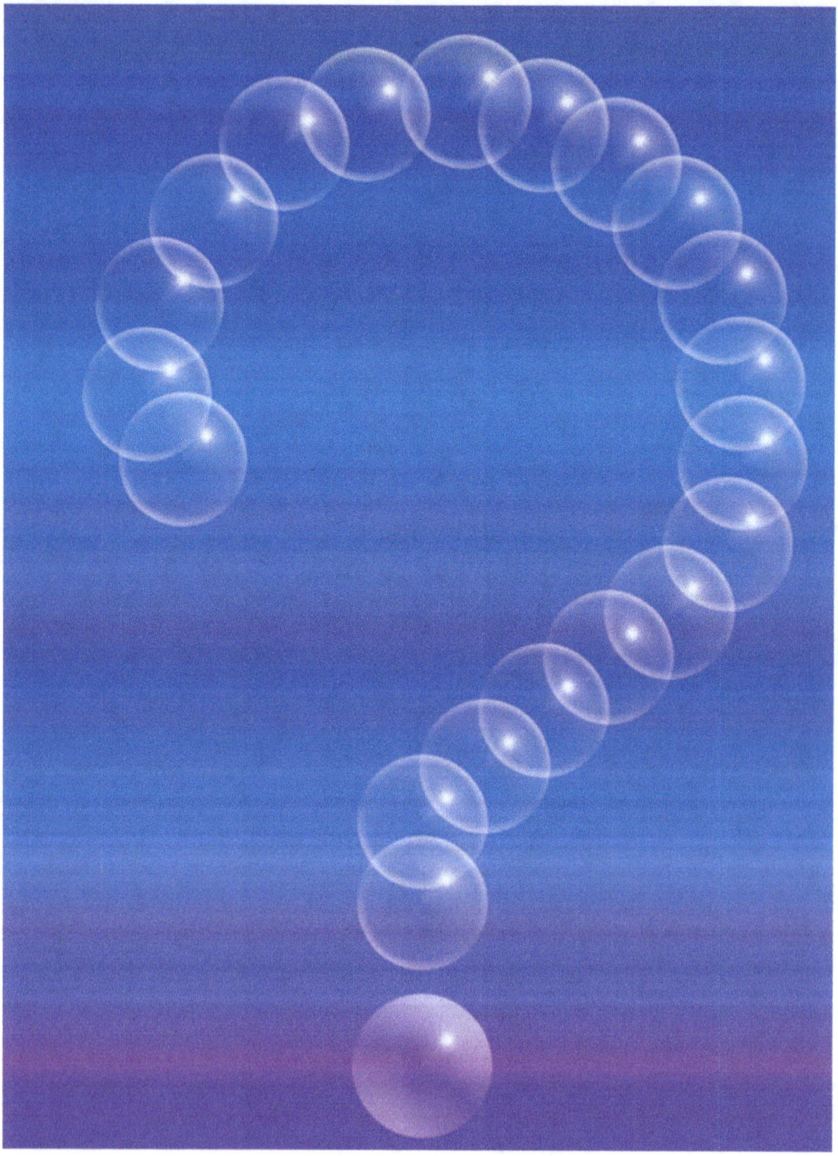

Is It True?

That all possessions get owned by those who did not create them

That man is only a reflection of God's corporeal ego

That the part only divides what yet remains whole

That woman has infinite capacity by design

That science cannot explain itself

That love is the child of God

That death is anti life

That life is a poem

That death awaits

For you

No?

Bold Colors

I woke to the sound of a cricket in the early morning light
Before the daily smell of life had put the flies in flight
A moment there, before I rose, ensconced in my cocoon
I pondered how to metamorphically escape my little womb

Today's the day to make myself a lady bug of sheer desire
With colors bright to catch the light, I worked on my attire
I flit about like a bumble bee, to make myself delicious
For all to see me naturally, and hardly surreptitious

Satisfied, I went outside, to cast my beauty as a butterfly
To wing about the vivid flowers might and wonder why
The caterpillar crawls and all the ants shop at the malls
To find their heart's desires, with tiny thoughts so small

Perhaps I take the risk of being eaten by a hungry bird
But not to take a chance in life, is absolutely just absurd

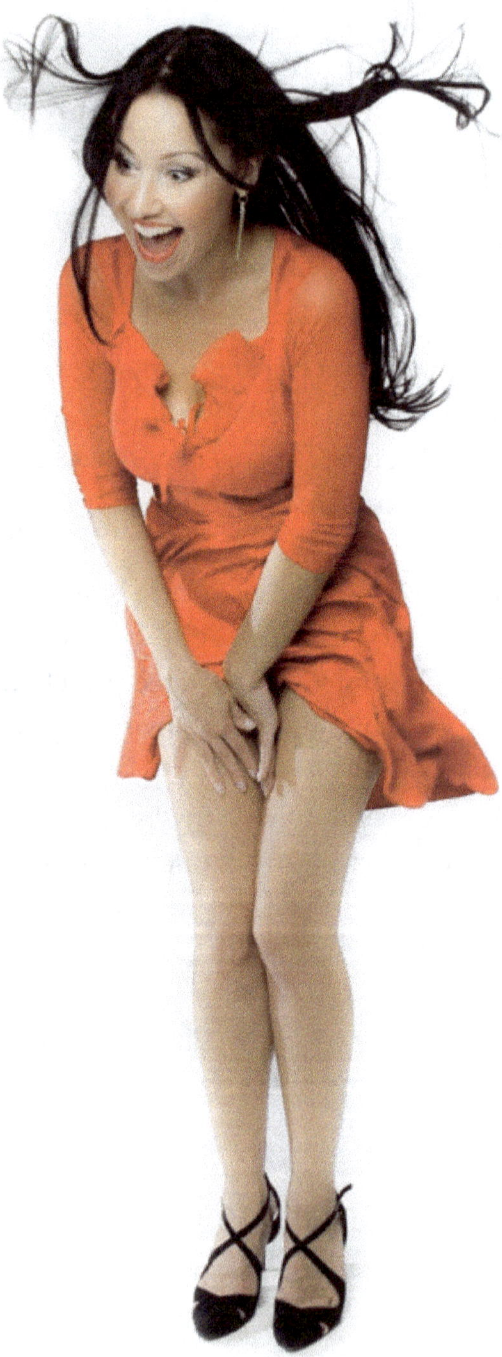

Just One Look

Frilly things that catch my eye do make me smile
Especially, when most attentively, I must surrender
Thoughts I had in mind, and lost to this contender
In the flicker of a moment, I could not reconcile
A reason not to look, that seemed to me worthwhile
Unashamedly I watched, to be the great defender
Of witnessing salaciously her show in all its splendor
For most assuredly I testify, the frilly thing had style

Consequences of this act should not be taken lightly
The sight you see can be the cause of your demise
To tread with caution, is the only way to brightly
Avoid a situation, where the intention is disguised
To lose your independent thought is quite unsightly
But desire trumping intellect, is simply no surprise

Graduation

And so pell-mell they all went into hell
With righteous good intentions
We watched 'em leave and wished them well
As products of our own invention

And so, oh well, as farmers in the dell
We stay behind, our fates have been decided
To watch them leave, yet still compelled
To have their needs provided

We sit and wait a spell, to listen for the bell
That rings, anticipating their return
We watched them leave and bid farewell
To the very soul of our concerns

To plant a seed and watch it grow
Is the greatest joy that one can know

The Merits of an Honest Effort

There came a time I realized I needed to support myself
And so I left my home and friends to strike it out alone
I had some cash to get me by and also youth and health
Somehow I knew inside of me, I never would go home
Alone I had within me, the seeds of independence sown

Five hundred miles passed before I found a place to stay
I looked until I found a room that seemed to me efficient
I needed time to find my mind and then arrange my day
I bought a paper, sought a job, at which I was proficient
I hated waiting tables, but then the money was sufficient

I figured I could save enough to dodge a pointless plight
To go in business for myself and prosper was my plan
And constantly a thought of mine and never out of sight
I finally saved enough to quit my job and take my stand
So carefully, I picked a place I felt I could command

For over thirty years, I was the captain of my destiny
Presiding over daily thoughts of gaining recognition
As profits came and went, I used them most propitiously
In trying to maintain a course, that by my own cognition
My efforts be not wasted, a product of my own volition

Now times are gone when I belonged to days of strife
Regrets I do not have at all, and with complete civility
I tried to make a difference in the way I spent my life
I surrendered up security and replaced it with integrity
So now I have prosperity, retaining my own dignity

To Dream Eternally

To ponder time while unencumbered
Of dreams that wander in by slumber
Reminding me to set my spirit free
Releasing it in peaceful dignity

Then quietly I rustled in my sleep
And silently I tussled just to keep
The aura wrapped around me tight
A light still trapped within the night

For gently I was floating on a cloud
Incidentally, quoting Keats out loud
So beautiful a dream had come to me
A joy forever more, not just a fantasy

It was as real as yesterday, I do insist
And certify indelibly my soul exists

Pliant Convictions

An opening line is always the best, to put a writer to the test
Of whether or not the work is worthy of the author's words
It begins with a bang and a clang from an inspiration stirred
Quite undeterred, yet unconfirmed, within the writer's breast

Attempts are made to weigh and save an inkling of surprise
In words provocatively picked, to entice the victim's mind
To understand, to take at hand, to assign the precious time
To acquire a way to not consign integrity to compromise

The text expounds around a truth the author has proposed
And contumaciously it calls, its premise to express its goals
It supplicates in great debate and aches to make it whole
To give its soul a reason to behold, as intendedly composed

A text is charged to, by and large, expound upon the theme
To never decree, to any degree, new revelations of its own
For in this realm and at the helm, Harmonia rules alone
As she is prone to not bemoan, the castigation of a dream

A premise stated cannot be abated, from its intended goal
Naturally born, it's then foresworn, to never stray far away
To cornerstone its continuity, to champion and hold at bay
Attempts conveyed to prey upon the righteousness extolled

The story told, the toll is paid, and the story is made to end
Perfection achieved it was decreed, indeed there isn't a flaw
The laws of literature had ruled, the work to be held in awe
But written laws are simply straw, for poets to transcend

A Solitary Tree

I saw a barren tree, alone upon a hill
Gnarled and twisted, it before the wind
Defiantly, in solitude, it stood still
Its spirit had no power to rescind
To bargain and regain its youth
For after all, it is the simple truth

Tenaciously, it weathered wind and rain
Its youthful beauty there for all to see
Alone, she lorded over her domain
Which did not bear another single tree
For miles around, she was the only one
A barren beacon, she had now become

For fifty years she flourished in her prime
Adored by all who sought her pulchritude
They came for inspiration all the time
To write of love in terms of certitude
Her doubtless majesty was loved by all
Who saw her standing there so tall

With accolades and eulogies they came
To share a moment with the lovely tree
To have their picture taken all in vain
Beneath its shade, in innocent simplicity
The people in the pictures did have names
But the tree had not, to no one's shame

It bore no fruit, so other trees could grow
No one thought to plant a mate beside it
Her seed had fallen aimlessly below
Her legacy of love was not provided
But fame and name yet came her way
For she was called, when her life had gone
The Hanging Tree of Nosegay

Diginnity

This chicken pie's divine
The farmer said with relish
Plenty chicken stuffed inside
He continued to embellish

It's work to make the dough
His wife said with delight
You roll it out real slow
And pinch the edges tight

It's the chickens work to eat
And that's the reason why
You also have to work
Or you shall have no pie

Hen Pecked

The chickens clucked about
Pecking for a juicy worm
Pecking until all pecked out
Until it was confirmed

The worms had run away
Not wanting to be pecked
Clucking now in great dismay
What did they all expect?

The worms to just endure
A clucking chicken pecking
They'd rather find manure
And off they went a trekking

A Liquid Refreshment

She wiggled her can from side to side
Oh, what a sight to see!
Back and forth she changed her stride
Oh, was it just for me?
She waggled around and did not hide
Oh, her femininity.
Then up and down she tried and tried
Oh, was it just for me?
In circles she gave, in a lavish supply
Oh, her generosity.
Then down it poured like a rainy sky
Oh my, it's not for me.
It was all for another, I couldn't deny
Oh, I could plainly see.
Yet I often remember her by and by
Oh,… so vividly.

Cause I never forgot how I felt like a man
Watching that girl with her watering can

To Have a Likeness to

I like it sunny when it's cold
I like it sunny when it's hot
I like it sunny when I'm old
I like it sunny when I'm not

I like the night with stars so bright
I like the night with darkness still
I like the night with pale moonlight
I like the night with peace at will

I like the spring as it appears
I like the summertime as well
I like the fall when it is here
I like in wintertime to dwell

But of all the things I like to be
I like to be a spirit free

To Scold Successfully

How pitiful she said to me, I had expected so much more
Of all the people that I know, your potential was the best
I feel you let me down, she said, you hurt me to the core
And so right now I feel you are, no better than the rest
Your poor performance cannot be from lack of my attention
Your failure to address yourself remains the only reason why
That if you don't apply yourself, it's by your own invention
And by your own invention then, you'll choose to live and die!

These words did stab me brutally, knowing they were true
I promise I'll repent my ways, admittedly because of you
Your efforts were relentless, and certainly respect is due
So don't abandon me right now, I'll try to change my ways
I promise you with certitude, your faith and love repay
For you will always be my mother, till the very end of days

Oh, For the Love of Spud

Everybody loves a good potato
At holidays you eat them mashed
You can fix them on your plate so
You can eat them unabashed

Some people build a gravy dam
And work to manage it with skill
To keep its essence from the yam
And o'er the corn that it would spill

Beaver dams do serve quite well
To engineer the thing you savor
The gravy you can always tell
Enhances the potato's flavor

So now you're stuffed, to no surprise
You dream of ketchup on your fries

Joy to the World

a Savior is Born

The Joy of Salvation

On golden harps the angels play to all the souls who lost their way
To all who felt complete despair, they bring a ray of hope to share
The song of joy that's sung this day, is sung for all who sit and pray
For God to help them as they bear a loss of faith with no compare

The faithful also feel the cheer, and each and everyone doth hear
As silver bells do surely ring, God's gift to man, the King of Kings
The holy angels fly so near, they do bring out the joyous tears
Reminding you of fragile things, that float about on angel's wings

For some a silent peace does fall, as others waken to the call
From hallelujah choirs, in white and golden robes attired
Do now proclaim to one and all, their sins forgiven, large and small
Rejoice with all your heart's desire, the love of Christ will never tire

Let salvation always be your goal, cast your worries from your soul
It's Christmastime, so just behold, the greatest story ever told

The Rural Life for Me

I wished to own a farm
And now I do, so I'll be darned
I married the schoolmarm
So she could teach me how
Exactly how to plow

To Taste Your Age

I knew that I had fallen in love the other day
Admittedly I was afraid, and verily I prayed
A ray of sunshine pierced my wanton heart
And notified my loneliness, - it best depart

In youth I loved at will, so readily it seemed
To fantasies that then were all but dreamed
Stipulations, nor regulations, were required
To sanctify and satisfy my wild heart's desire

The possibility that I would gain once more
The faded ecstasies once felt in days of yore
This love is tempting, I can't believe it's true
An unrepentant passion, appearing all anew

In vain, I'm going to try again, to be or not to be
True, to a new recipe, that boasts its sugar free!

Think About It

A sky without a cloud is loud
A bank is not a straight shot
A home is never in one place
A pile is the result of a hole
The earth is made of earth
Pies are made to be eaten
A horse is not a cow
A shovel can't
Man can
Female is
Love is nice
Why is a circle
Me is adversity
Hate is despicable
All words are feeble
We is always wanting
Peace is an acquisition
Nature refuses to obey
Your funny bone is not
All tunes are orchestrated
Escape is almost probable
Hair is always where it's at
Spirits defy centrifugal force
Sight is good, but insight is better
Thought without action is loneliness
Average is smaller than insignificance

The Write Advice

I'm here for you to write upon
Before your thought's all gone
Don't hesitate to write it down
Don't vacillate or fool around
To have to say, "I can't recall"
Displays a mind so very small
To lose a thought is oh so sad
If only you had this little pad!

Degradation Incarnate

The highest accolades were given
By notable officials there
As self aggrandizement was driven
With noses in the air

They claimed the moral high ground
Anointed by their board
Their noble prize was so profound
You'd die for their award

Now that's a thought that's worthy,
A notable had said
We'll give them cash deservedly
And notify the dead

I think this thought is dynamite
We'll catch them unaware
We'll award the prize to someone
Who has nothing to declare

They all agreed to this award
Professing to be wise
By trashing all who came before
To politically arise

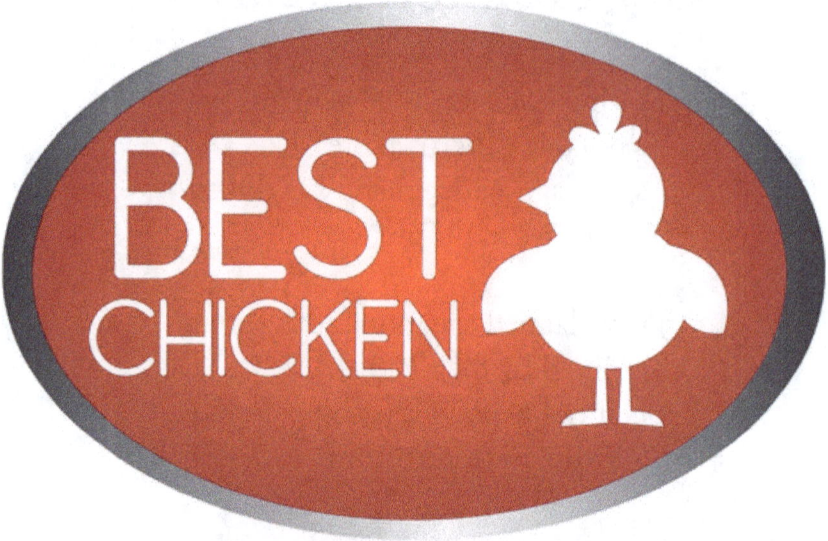
BEST
CHICKEN

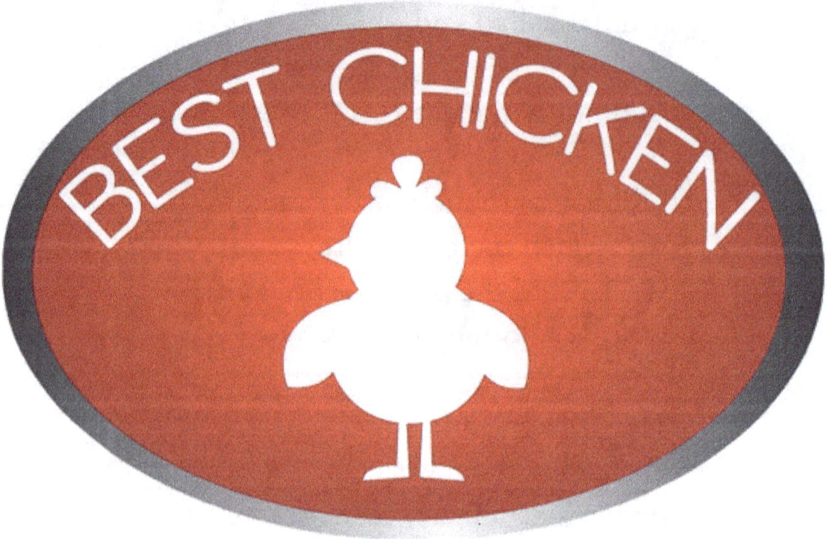
BEST CHICKEN

Fameininity

The egg was laid with joy
Laid in the nest with care
With happiness employed
But no one else was there

The hen did cackle loudly
The others ought to know
Again she cackled proudly
My egg's the best of show

She advertised her fame
To everyone ambitiously
And then the weasel came
And ate her egg deliciously

Inherent Independence

Wonder what it's like to be alive?
Wake each day, expecting just to be
A new creation, there for all to see
The sense of exaltation now arrives
Unfettered passion in the heart arise
Anticipate experience with ecstasy
And be yourself without impunity
Embrace your life without disguise

Beware endearing efforts to conform
To feel accepted as your life's reward
Souls cannot be bound in uniforms
Your sprit's a song you can't record
Forever it will always be foresworn
You'll ponder how integrity is born

Excogitate Your Ride

I love my car
It's where I are
Wherever I may go

It gets me there
And then I'm where
My carcass is in tow

So down the road
I take my load
And drive another mile

I don't care why
The other guy
Just doesn't ride in style

But as for me
You clearly see
My car is so worthwhile

For all of you who can't relate
And just accept your fickle fate
Of this I must articulate

You need to know
Don't ride too slow
Or I will steal the show

Undying Love

I pretended not to lie, just as she pretended to believe me
She said she was a pear, existing out there, all by herself
She hung herself without affair, so neatly and discreetly
Her body swung in perfumed air, poignantly yet sweetly
I took her down and put her there, upright upon a shelf
As I do swear, I even dared, that she improve her health

She changed her mind relentlessly, by every single day
And changed her scent religiously, reliably quite daily
But never did she ask to change her clothes in any way
She begged me let her down, and promised not to stray
She then concertedly amused me, cavorting oh so gaily
But sadly dancing all around, she fell about most frailly

She wouldn't eat at any time, no matter what was made
And soon it was apparent, her figure had become too thin
I hung her back upon the tree that stood outside the glade
Her happiness returned, while back and forth she swayed
I knew she loved it there when she revealed that little grin
Her love for me now unconcealed, as it had never been

A Whale of a Time

```
              fro                      little
         and       and            my       boat
      to              to    fro              did
So                and                           go
         side                took
       to    the               and    away
      side        boat    ride               my
And                did                        pride
           and                from
       down    up         went    hight
      and           and    I              to
Up                down                        low
           know                just
         to    when            it's  your
       need          "Thar she blows!"      lunch
You                                          inside
```

Heed in Deed

Does a spirit know its fate?
Intangibles they are
Erasable at any rate
The thought is so bizarre

Are they in fact anomalies?
Impossible to know
Effectively it's only me
Their therapy I undergo

They speak to me in certitude
That it will come to pass
And I believe they do allude
That karma does amass

Alone it's me I must decide
Intangibles in fact exist
To let my conscious be my guide
Not fall in the Abyss

It's obvious, I'm not there now
And I don't want to be
But as for you, I pity you
If you refuse your therapy

Fleedom

Cock a doodle do
The rooster called to me
What was I to do?
Surrender unequivocally

I'm a free range chicken
Not part of any flock
I roam to my convictions
His bantering's a crock

The chicken feed implored
To live in a chicken coop
Is something so abhorred
I'd rather be chicken soup

Optimism

I can't smell with my nose
I can't see where I goes
I can't touch my toes
I can't taste one of dose
And I'm deaf, I suppose

But I'm getting better!

A Full Palette

Life explodes in a blinding white
From the colorless void we come
Conceived beyond our very sight
The void's remanded to succumb

Then yellow bursts upon the scene
With vibrant golden beams of light
The breath of life inside does seem
To warm you with a God's delight

Midst orange flairs and scarlet red
We touch the heaven's surly might
With caution gone we surely tread
Convinced we truly have the right

When green's sereneness filters in
No longer are you bound so tight
You now express the soul within
And redefine your natural plight

Enjoy the blues with all their hues
Their comforting but not as bright
Revere your past and sit and muse
For nature's peace you now invite

As royal shades of purple fade
And candles flicker in the night
My colored life I'd never trade
For me it's been a true delight

A Poet's Epitaph

You can try to fly so high, to escape the rules of why
You are the seagull that you are

You pity an old man, fishing all his life to understand
That it's the worm that wins

You can try to build a fire, to rekindle your desires
And wish upon a star

Your plantation's all but gone, to Nature's final song
While ants play violins

For all we're gonna do is... go naturally

An Irish Lassie

For I'm a Scott and I fear not
Until I met an Irish Girl
She was so beautiful

With hair of red, she all but said
I am but life itself
She was so beautiful

Her purpose was for all to see
Herself in all her glory
She was so beautiful

And she will always be to me
So beautiful

I Ain't an Ant!

The ant trail was congested,
Or was I being tested?
Was I in line?
Was I behind?
About to be molested?

Should I simply just speed up?
Or perhaps I should slow down?
Maybe surrender?
Nolo contendere?
Or prepare to leave the town?

Oh my God, what do I see?
Is that another ant by me?
Trying to escape?
Fearing to be raped?
Yielding all integrity?

Do you think that it is wise?
Will it hasten my demise?
To now confess?
Like all the rest?
And just pay homage to the hive?

The Snowman Cometh

The sky is lit in twinkling lights of fragile thoughts of hope
Glistening o'er a snow so bright, as snowflakes verily elope
With childhood dreams that reappear, joyously in splendor
Awakening those days of old, all but forgotten in surrender

Innocence is never lost, becoming dormant in compliance
Initially a frost is felt, confronting now your own defiance
Embrace the Snowy Angels, resurrect your childhood past
Reject that Merry Old Snowmen, are never expected to last

Christmas Carols call to thee, to now surrender, unequivocally
Deny the hierarchy created by society, find virtue in simplicity
Rejoice the vestal nature of a child, God's gift you can revive
And certify to all who'll listen, that snowmen are indeed alive

L'eggalese

Hello my feathered friend
You need my help today?
It's the chickens I defend
Now let's discuss my pay

A chicken has its rights
I know the chicken laws
For you I'll duly fight
For scratch upon my craw

So the fox had guaranteed
She would perhaps survive
Sadly tho' he never agreed
He wouldn't eat her pride

Prosperity

Delicate orchids
Envision a taste of love
For you to feast on

This Old House

My house was old but comfortable
I mused reclining in my chair
With fondest memories it was full
Of all that had transpired there
In repairing all its wear and tear

To keep it looking just the same
As I had hoped that it would stay
Forever pictured in a frame
Just as it was that very day
I knew I couldn't walk away

It's maintenance, the builder said
Do not give in to negligence
Do not neglect your overhead
For that's the cause of decadence
And you will lose your residence

Whoever comes to take my place
The moment that they sign the deed
The truest thing they'll have to face
The one thing that is guaranteed
It's maintenance they better heed

GRAMMAR

You're Going Nowhere

I'm present said the participle to the verb
To be somewhere without me is absurd
You can always change your tense in time
To in the future hide
Or in the past reside
But as it is right now, you must remain all mine!

The Omnipotent Book

Ouch! I cried,
As it snapped closed upon my hand,
Then silence fell.

Ah Hah! I thought,
You failed to dominate my mind,
I'll never tell.

Heh Heh! I mused,
For I was in complete control,
My soul to keep.

Oh No! I feared,
I forgot to mark my place,
How can I sleep?

Ha Ha! I heard,
When once again I opened it,
You can't resist.

He He! It laughed,
You have to read me now again,
I must insist.

Or you will never know.

Be Yourself, Damn It!

Why would anyone want to stay inside?
The weather's great out here, I must confide
It is a perfect day to take a ride
Then to decide, inside you cannot hide

How long have you been hiding in this way?
And not enjoy the seizure of this day
The essence of your life, a sweet bouquet
You stifle there, and swear in sad decay

Come out, come out, I know you are within!
I call you out, dismissing your chagrin
You have to learn to take it on the chin
It's no one now but thou, who's giving in

For you and you alone, have to decide
To finally let your conscience be your guide

Eaten Alive

Alone my mortality is
Heightened by my fall
And thus secured within
My racing mind
My eyes are blind
For they refuse to see
Neither do I want to hear
My own stupidity
The noxious smell
Could overcome a goat
There is my nose
When I don't want it most
Right now I have no taste
For sex in any form
The molars crush
The touch within me

Hello

High I am, today
Hi, I am today

Souplexed

Chicken soup you need
To chase this cold away
And hardily I guarantee
I'll make it all the way

Egg noodles make it nice
And carrots give it flavor
As herbs will give it spice
A treat for you to savor

It's quite a healthy remedy
Whenever you are stricken
It's a cure for all humanity
But deadly to the chicken

Darnel Knowledge

I think a child I'll always be, but never again a boy
To wonder most incredibly the things I now employ
To keep me free of drudgery, the very enemy of life
The things I wanted to achieve, the object of my strife

To be a king or president, I thought when I was young
Would be the answer to my dreams, and also lots of fun
Then I read of kingly Lear and saw the fate of Kennedy
As Burnham's Wood was near enough to host insanity

I had the princess of my dreams, my very heart's desire
As I was in my boyish state, I never felt my ardor tire
Then came along Ben Franklin, varieties the spice of life
So now it's grand vacations, and just to please my wife

If I could only start a business, I'd surely be a millionaire
A Lincoln Log constructor, or architect extraordinaire
But then I read The Fountainhead, I did not like the end
To survive for wanton power, I'd surely be condemned

I could always be a doctor with intelligence to spare
There were always plenty Barbies, in need of sad repair
But then I read of Bovary, where ineptitude abounds
Feeling empathy for Emma, I too would leave the town

And so, I've lost my boyish dreams and toys that I adored
To be a literary child, where all my faults are underscored

Poetry Can Be

Thoughtfully inductive so sublime
Inceptively corruptive by design
Mentally seductive just like wine
Discerningly eruptive as a crime
Socially conductive all entwined
Tauntingly obstructive to the mind
Randomly deductive as assigned
Hopefully productive, be it mine
Deliberately destructive unaligned
Philosophically adductive any time
Certainly instructive most refined
Elusively constructive so inclined
Easily reproductive when supine
Wholly interruptive unconfined
Gratefully instructive in your prime
Fiscally unproductive most the time

Dogged Notions

I thought the other day, it made me quite perturbed
Why it is so definitive that dog is man's best friend
And I be treated differently, it got me quite disturbed
That I should only have a cat is what they recommend
For I would be an oddity, if I should buck the trend

My independence with me, I went to seek a pet
It told me quite exclusively, I only need to satisfy
My own desires solely, and other notions just forget
As I surveyed the store, a little doggy caught my eye
Take me, it sighed most dolefully, as I advanced nearby

I make my own decisions too, and surely I pick you
The little dog cajoled me in a most delicious way
I won't eat a lot, it told me, and I'll love you oh so true
And from my heart, I swear to you, I'll never ever stray
So believing this succumbing, I picked him up that day

When I come home from work, he'll run around my feet
He'll dance around the room to amuse me even more
And then while standing up, he'll beg me for a treat
And follow me intently right through the kitchen door
And show me unashamedly, exactly where they're stored

Then sitting in my chair at night, he cradles in my lap
To listen to me share the tribulations of the night
Together we compare our nature not to be entrapped
By rules and regulations that do nothing but incite
Definitive affirmations– that never see the light

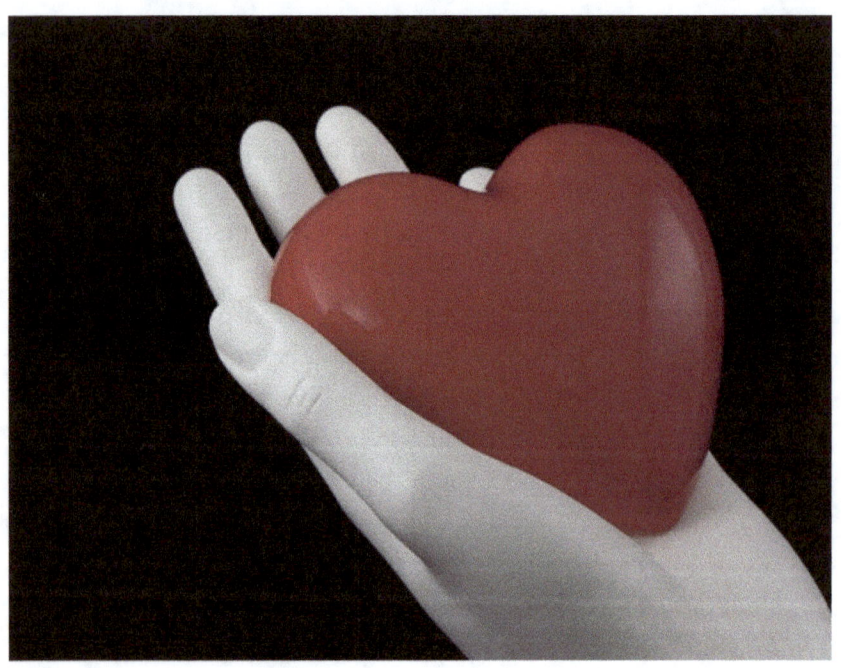

Complete Surrender

It is your love that makes me feel alive
Your tender kisses weaken me inside
As I surrender to you soft caress
My heart's forever yours I must confess

You took me by surprise as I gave in
To wanton feelings I had hid within
So now I'm paralyzed and naked too
And all because I fell in love with you

My passion has consumed my very soul
To once again love you, my only goal
Take me now, don't leave me in this way
To not receive the rapture of this day

Your love's a pleasure I can't live without
You are my love, and all what I'm about

The Hunk of Funk

I tried the Funky Chicken
Cause I wanted to be cool
So I could have my pickin
Of all the chicks at school

I strutted and I bantered
As funky chickens do
So I could be the dancer
Admired by the brood

So I became impeccable
A classic piece of work
Unlike the other imbeciles
Who tried to do the Jerk

Flight School

Don't throw in the towel, said the wise old owl
If nothing is ventured, then nothing is gained
To have an adventure, and not run afoul
You need to fly right, you need to be trained

As the little bird listened, his eyes opened wide
His feathers a flutter, he danced all around
When he couldn't decide, he got queasy inside
And worried to death, he'd fall to the ground

He looked down below, the tree was so high
The branches were there to ruin his flight
He looked up above, there was nothing but sky
But felt in his soul, he did not have it right

He then cautiously went to the edge of the nest
And finally was met with a rear-ended boot
While flapping about, he passed his first test
While all the time thinking, his teacher's a brute

He flitted and floated, not far did he roam
And struggled profusely to stay in the air
Endeavored he fought to make it back home
To enjoy once again, the security there

He landed exhausted, and he slipped and he fell
As he flew through the nest like a bat out of hell
He realized then, there was no other route
And the stoic old coot, ...really did give a hoot

Sport

I have discerned, she was well turned
Oh, I did yearn; I felt that I had earned, a ride

And then I learned, I might be spurned
And might be burned and not returned, alive

So unconcerned, the jury did return
And then affirmed and did confirm, and sighed

Incredibly, I briefly died

A Temporal Reception

It was the rain that made the tin roof come alive
The pitter-patter sound I hear when they collide
Within my senses deep inside, I verily proclaim
It caused my soul a great concern, I couldn't hide

A hideous seditious rot around my window frame
My window to the world would never be the same
Unsecured, the pane of glass it loosely held inside
Might fall upon the ground to break and not retain

The thoughts that my integrity had held with pride
So privately within my mind, they were my guide
My personal desires, held in my sanctified domain
In dreams of mine that I alone, in solitude preside

For rain can be a blessing, or seem a curse as well
Sanctioned out of Heaven or be the wrath of Hell

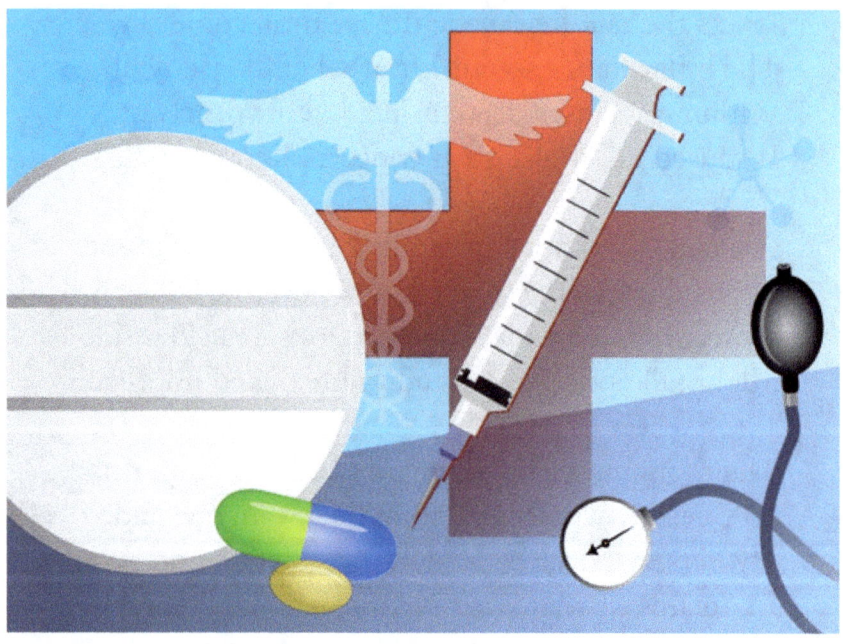

Rampant Stupidity

Diabetes, I pee on thee; I like my sugar sweet
For years I've always had my way
With stamps aplenty, to buy my treats
Not having to work, to get my pay
The man will heal me now, I do declare
For I receive O'Bubba Care

Jeannie

You will always be there
With your chestnut hair
Past shoulders where
Your belly was bare
Under riblets above
Thrusting with love
Over low-cut jeans
Tight at the seams
God calls to me
From eternity
To hold on tight
With all my might
To a love so strong
It is never so long
I go not thinking
About you

With No Help From My Friends

I built myself a Throne
So I could be the King
Because I was unknown
I had to build this thing

I wasn't born a Prince
To inherit me this job
Alone, I build it since
I was just another slob

The Legacy Left Behind

People used to get about on foot
Wandering about, refusing to stay put
Cleverly, they used a horse's back
Vowing to return to 'this old shack'

Horses led the way to iron trains
Chugging folks away from their domain
Professing love with great concern
Stating, 'someday soon' they will return

Venturing where trains can't roam
The automobile took folks from home
And going away, I heard them say
'Don't worry, I'll be back some day'

For heritage lost remains a pity
The term is now, The Inner City

Reverent Elation

Easter Eggs were hidden with care
In hallowed places everywhere
In flower meadows they were placed
And blessed by God, in all His grace

A joy for children to discover
That Jesus lives in one another
As all their sins were washed away
When Jesus Christ arose that day

In faith the children look around
For love and guidance to be found
Each egg uncovered, one by one
Reveals his love to everyone

Whenever spirits soar on high
The Son of God is right nearby

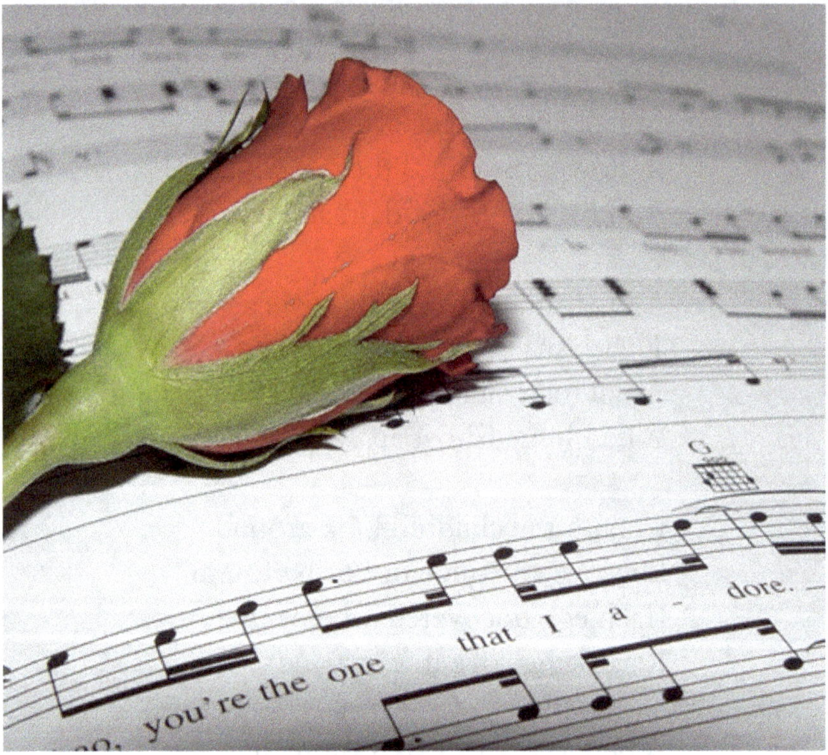
G
you're the one that I a - dore.

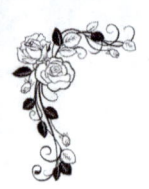

Wholly in Love

You made me feel empty
And I could not pretend
I could not understand
I could not comprehend
The instant you took me
There was nothing inside
You gave me a passion
I could no longer hide

For only to love you, is all that I feel
Since the second I saw you, you made my life real
Come here to me gently, I surrender my soul
So we can be lovers, so we can be whole

I feel you inside me
You will never be gone
And lying beside me
Is a beautiful song
With ardor I play thee
On your love I do thrive
You make me feel happy
For you make me alive

For only to love you, is all that I feel
Since the second I saw you, you made my life real
Come here to me gently, I surrender my soul
So we can be lovers, so we can be whole

Nutrition Facts

Serving Size 1/6 package (60g)
Servings Per Container 6

Amount Per Serving	Mix	Prepared
Calories	260	360
Calories from Fat	80	150
	% Daily Value*	
Total Fat 9g*	14%	26%
Saturated Fat 3.5g	18%	30%
Cholesterol 0mg	0%	1%
Sodium 360mg	15%	20%
Total Carbohydrate 46g	15%	16%
Dietary Fiber 1g	4%	4%
Sugars 28g		
Protein 2g		
Vitamin A	0%	10%
Vitamin C	0%	0%
Calcium	15%	25%
Iron	6%	6%

*Amount in mix
Daily Values are based on a 2,000

Treat Yourself

The package said it had fantastic flavor
It was packed with nutrients aplenty
It guaranteed a treat that I would savor
Enticing all my senses quite intensely

I took it from the shelf to read acutely
Exactly what was secretly delicious
I found a list and read it most astutely
Proclaiming all ingredients nutritious

O M G it had some chocolate inside it
And salt enhancing my appreciation
The sugar told me that I had to try it
It seduced me, this best of all creations

For it's the natural essence of a snack
To satisfy your cravings in a sack

Hire Me!

They paid for my college
And my degree does acknowledge
I wasn't a stupil pupil

Allured

Music was there
Beneath her breath
I could feel it
Upon my neck
T'was in her hair
Intertwined
Tuned in time
A breeze so fine
Bade me not
Resist
Play with me
She tickled
Wistfully so
Gently I did
Succumb
To then become
At peace with love

Smokezy

You know by crakie
I love my tobacckie
It makes me happie
When I feel crappie

Just Desserts

The bomb went off, then silence fell
As horror rose, right up from hell
Forsaken and completely stirred
God save my soul, the cry was heard

Then condemnation was proclaimed
You're lucky you were only maimed
A righteous man had said to me
The body count is high you see

You should be grateful, you survived
And thankful that you're still alive
I promise, we will find the ones
And give you justice when we're done

They apprehended all involved
And vowed to all, they were resolved
They would receive their just desserts
But they have rights, they did assert

If only we just feed them pie
They'll have remorse and wonder why
They slaughter other human beings
Because they simply disagree

The righteous folks were quite amused
They never stood inside my shoes
And, Oh my country 'tis of thee
They gave them apple pie to eat!

Trick or Treat

He was a treat I have to say, deliciously he came my way
Oblivious I was before, but now I thought I would explore
His obvious intentions, which I could not ignore
And I was oh so bored

He wanted to consume me, to wound me and entomb me
To whisk away my defense, to subdue my effervescence
His boldness had no pretense, which fed his very offense
For he was quite intense

I was at home, not all alone, entering my twilight zone
My stranger still in tow, his intentions all aglow
He petulantly crowed, of what he could bestow
As if I didn't know

A little wine, a little time, for inhibitions to subside
He was a credit to his kind, a beast of burden so inclined
To do the task he was assigned, surrendering his mind
The victim of his crime

Alas he had grown old to me, no more a curiosity
His function terminated, for which he was created
His essence subjugated, his future now was slated
As only death awaited

You see he had to pay, and bade me not delay
Forgive me he had pled, when chained upon my bed
For I rather now be dead, than be inside your head
A cruel trick, he said

Vote Yourself a Job

Good job, bad job, no job at all, you have to have a task
But how much will you pay me, just to sit upon my ass?

Good pay, bad pay, no pay at all, you cannot buy your dignity
If this you don't believe, how much money do you need?

Good man, bad man, no man at all, this contract is contemptible
Don't find this reprehensible? To whom is it acceptable?

The Complaint Department

Hold it there, said the scissors to the hair
Before you grow any more
Flying here and there, giving me despair
You make this job a chore!

The brush spoke up, and made it known
It wasn't happy either
This client's hair I do declare, has grown
In matted, like a beaver's!

Frankly, I hate the state of my condition
Spoke up the lowly cape
No one ever wants to cover my position
So nastily, I suffocate!

What about the chair? -they always squirm
Do I not have a voice?
For asses' fat and skinny, I suffer to intern
And never have a choice!

Whenever you listen to another complain
You become their tool of cursing in vane!

To Nestle

There was a little chickie
Who had the cutest peep
I knew it would be tricky
And certainly not cheap

I had to save my scratch
For I didn't want to beg
This relationship to hatch
And not just lay an egg

Alas, I built a lovely nest
Feathered soft with down
And feeling truly blessed
She finally stuck around

Travel Arrangements

What will I do with myself, whenever I have to leave
And what about you, when you have to leave as well
I don't want to think of it now
It'll work itself out some how
But without my love beside me, I cannot say farewell

Come with me now and we will adventure together
To choose the course that'll tie our dreams to a star
I have never ridden a train
And certainly wouldn't complain
But with you at my side, I'd ride in the baggage car

Surly you know, that here we can no longer stay
The sound of the past cries out loud at the station
I cannot leave you behind
My love, I cannot resign
If I travel alone, -this love will die of starvation

Give unto me, the love that I need to sustain me
To journey from here together in passionate love
So you, I tenderly kiss
And place upon your lips
The song of joy that flys on the wings of a dove

A train might be fine to leave my worries behind
But this love makes me soar, to the heavens galore

New Age Thought

You notice not the fly before the sex
It's ever presence there had no effect
Before, it's just a speck upon the wall
But after, it's a nuisance - be it small

You wonder just exactly what it saw
Ponder what conclusions it would draw
From a performance held most privately
That wasn't meant for viewing, publicly

Content you know a fly can't speak
Of what it saw, in taking just a peek
Then you think, -well I'll be damned
Perchance it owns a tiny little cam?

Swat this thing, you now conclude!
Before you're seen on You Tube…

Always

I often wonder
Where you are
The part of you
Outside of me
The part of you
In others
And what is left
Dissipation never rests
Perhaps in other interests
But not of you in me

To Run Afowl

The chickens ran around
Their little hearts apanic
A ticket had been found
For a ride on the Titanic

Perched high I saw it all
A rooster said with pride
Its curtains for you all
The trailer did decry

It's coming soon to you
It certianily conveyed
And nothing you can do
To pray this fact away

Standing Ground

I am the grey that comes from black
The finest marble still has cracks
That light itself intensifies

From shadows deep inside our souls
Our thoughts are forged as black as coal
Escaping, just like fireflies

When hammered hot within your mind
The sparks of knowledge you will find
Fly out before your very eyes

From total darkness into light
In shades of grey you gain insight
From wisdom that before you lies

The bust of Socrates decries
It is ignorance you must defy

Expose Yourself

Who are you to read my poem
Expecting to invade my home
Its sanctity right on display
To catch my soul in disarray

You feed upon the negative
You only take and never give
Integrity you call your own
But never wrote a single poem

Repulsively on love you feast
You hideous demonic priest
And gorge yourself on ridicule
You nasty literary ghoul

I know that I will never see
A critic with a soul to be

A Fine Confection

Wanda was a sumptuous tart
Delicious, right from the start
For God dressed her in lace
And gave her great taste
And then filled her chock full of heart

Positively Fine

There once was a girl named Sandy
Everyone thought she was candy
When you had a frown
And felt outright down
Her presence was always quite handy

Finely Tuned

There once was a girl named Vicki
Who was never known for a quickie
For she had infinite wisdom
For all to envision
And assuredly, she was most picky

Encore

A Homeric Tale of the Ages

The Marriage of Mother Nature

A Grecian Mini Epic

Innocence is born in brilliant glory, unspoiled and unashamed
The initial breath of every story, endeavoring to be acclaimed
Experience, in quiet stealth, awaits for Fame to gain its prize
As Harmony adjudicates, and Father Time doth supervise

It has forever been this way, evoked and spoke Tradition
Well, I'm so bored I snored the other day, declared Ambition
And I agree, Enthusiasm did decree, it is a party that we need
So, someone summon Hermes, and proceed with Godly speed

A marriage, Aphrodite did demand, we need a party planned
I will have to call on Eros, and seek his expeditious hand
Let Zeus decide the bride, we'll need his blessing to proceed
A bride that we can be assured, a willing groom will please

Mother Nature was the nominee, the essence of Humanity
To resist her awesome beauty, would simply prove insanity
Father Time is easily amused, tho never thinks of marriage
But a natural timeless wife to woo, he never could disparage

The Harvest Queen may not be pleased, the Vanities suggested
She's far too beautiful for him they teased, and verily attested
For Old Man time is far from prime, he's always been so grim
Tempestuously bold they did surmise, she'll never marry him

Then Hermes spoke, this is no joke, we have to have a plan
Persephone I feel perhaps, can make her mother understand
I'll have to deal with Hades, to bargain for his cloistered lady
I think he'll deal with Father Time, they're both a little shady

Mother Nature is strong, and won't go along with this match
The Nymphs decreed, yet still agreed, she was indeed a catch
But Eros' quiver may not deliver, enough to blind her mind
To Persephone and Dionysus, this enterprise we should assign

Hermes concurred and then was heard to say he'd take the task
To invite Demeter to a feast, that even Time could not outlast
Reluctantly, she accepted the meal, despite his reputation known
Hephaestus forged the dirty deal, the seeds of Deceit were sown

The trumpets played and tables displayed a cornucopia of food
A command was sent for the great event, not to attend was rude
Tradition arrived, ascribed and assigned the necessary positions
Ceremony showed and all but glowed, in stating her conditions

The bride, indeed, is never to see the groom before the wedding
Secrecy was there to conceal, the direction they were aheading
The Furies concurred, her mind must be blurred and compliant
If she finds out, what it's all about, she'll only become defiant

A glass of wine before they dined was determined to be correct
A toast to Zeus, it was deduced, was to be offered with respect
Dionysus selected, was hence elected, to serve the bride to be
A special wine with herbs sublime to act in time, most potently

Inhibition was there but gave up Care, once drinking a libation
The Muses played and all were swayed, embracing procreation
Then readily aloft, both hard and soft, the golden arrow struck
The aim of Eros tried and true, and Mother Nature out of luck

Persephone had purposely, been placed right by her side
Then Hermes came and told her, your mother is the bride
Having never had a husband, and this her golden chance
Her daughter whispered quietly, she should accept a dance

What harm could be, to pleasantly, engage propitiously in fun
To take a chance and gain romance, is surely good for everyone
Now Father Time, first being in line, he asked her for her hand
And when she accepted, she never suspected, so devious a plan

The moment he held her, she fainted away from the spell
As he took her away, that festive day, he bid them all farewell
Now Ares provided the way, and secured them a place to stay
Where Father Time could cache her, safely sheltered away

When Mother Nature awoke, she only spoke of Persephone
Oh daughter, my virtue is slaughtered, for this cannot be me
I can't be this, an old goat's tryst, I have to attend to Man
Seek Hera's advice, pay any price, and help me if you can

Disarmed by the charm of Eros, she was robbed of all volition
To be supine with Father Time, was never her own position
He's old and cold and smells of mould, she eminently thought
For now behold, I am controlled, and in this spell I'm caught

So into the valley of Tempe, he brought his bride to hide
His treasure there he kept, from all suspicious prying eyes
The hills of Arcady were there, replete in awesome splendor
As he commanded tempus fugit, to gain complete surrender

And so he kept her locked away, and bade her stay inside
Perhaps she'd still be there today, if not for little butterflies
They flitted all about her room, the moment he had gone
Allegiantly they swore to her, that help will come along

What have I done! Persephone outrageously decried
I've been taken in by Hermes, he's trickery personified
The butterflies reminded her, that Eros did the dirty deed
And philtred wine gave him the time, to actually succeed

To Hera she went in audience, to salvage her mother's pride
To clearly hear through tiny tears the lament of the butterflies
As Hera was told of this plan so bold, she furiously blew up
For a party for Zeus, for fun and abuse, is scurrilously corrupt

My husband has gone too far, and someone is going to pay
To Man, Demeter's a star, and I'm going to keep it that way
Athena will help us Persephone, and Hestia will help us too
As sisters we'll call Harmony, she'll know just what to do

So a meeting took place, and they all did embrace an escape
We can take her away clandestinely, cloaked in the Aegis Cape
Athena the wise to no surprise came up with a brilliant scheme
For even Father Time has dreams, and this will be our means

Morpheus I know will help, so we can count on his support
For he can camouflage himself, according to my last report
While Father Time is dreaming, of Morpheus being Demeter
The Aegis Cape is her escape, her freedom from this Reaper

Hestia now had solemnly vowed, to bow in total devotion
To Gaia she prayed to give this day, a blessing to her potion
If Eros' charm is doing harm, its purpose has lost its soul
And this secret pact must stay intact, or fail to reach its goal

With this advice they all allied, to conjure the secret brew
The butterfly tears, sincere and dear, began the potent stew
Next was added a lock of hair, taken right from Psyche's lair
For if Eros ever lost Psyche, it'd be more that he could bear

Assured the cure would endure, they added a grain of sand
From an hour glass in ages past, belonged to Thee Old Man
Persephone volunteered to take the God of Dreams in hand
And righteously and faithfully, complete the task as planned

The butterflies rejoiced that day, the moment she was released
Persephone shed tears of joy, the instant the torture had ceased
As her Mother awoke she instantly spoke, I have to take a bath
And when I'm done, everyone....will suffer the pain of Wrath

Aphrodite and Eros are fated forever to only be a valentine
And Hermes idea of speed will inventively run out of time
Dionysus shall feel the lack of appeal, to be revealed a skunk
Nobility gone, he'll always long, for a time he wasn't a drunk

For Zeus and his Cronies and Father Time, Mankind will retire
To be banished to Mount Olympus, to never again be admired
Now Mother Nature will survive, and the Age of Man continue
On every Earth Day she's revived, but as a God, she bid adieu

But Gods never ever, forever and ever, go quietly into the night
For by way of design they left behind, the very concept of Spite
When Father Time had lost his prize, he cursed Man in despise
The plague of age he'll suffer in pain, until his ultimate demise

~ *Fin* ~

www.ingramcontent.com/pod-product-compliance
Lightning Source LLC
Chambersburg PA
CBHW070942230426
43666CB00011B/2529